Living Values Parent Groups:
A Facilitator Guide

# Living Values Parent Groups: A Facilitator Guide

Diane Tillman

**Health Communications, Inc.**
**Deerfield Beach, Florida**

*www.hci-online.com*

Visit the Living Values Web site for trainings at *http://www.livingvalues.net.*

**Library of Congress Cataloging-in-Publication Data**

Tillman, Diane
    Living Values parent groups: a facilitator guide / Diane Tillman.
      p.   cm.
    ISBN 1-55874-882-2 (trade paper)
    1. Parenting—Study and teaching.   2. Values—Study and teaching.   I. Title.

  HQ755.7.T56 2000
  649'.1'071—dc21

                                                    00-063453

Living Values: An Educational Program is a partnership among educators around the world. This program is supported by UNESCO and sponsored by the Spanish Committee of UNICEF, the Planet Society, and the Brahma Kumaris, in consultation with the Educational Cluster of UNICEF (New York).

HCI, its Logos and Marks are trademarks of Health Communications, Inc.

Publisher:  Health Communications, Inc.
           3201 S.W. 15th Street
           Deerfield Beach, FL 33442-8190

*Cover redesign and inside book design by Lawna Patterson Oldfield*
*Cover artwork by Frow Steeman*
*Cover design by David Warrick-Jones*
*Original Editors: Carol Gill, Gayatri Naraine, Diana Beaver*

*To my
Mother and Father,
wonderful parents
and examples.*

# CONTENTS

## OVERVIEW

## SECTION 1: THE GROUP PROCESS

## SECTION 2: PARENT VALUES ACTIVITIES

## SECTION 3: PARENTING SKILLS

# OVERVIEW

Parents, educators and more and more children are increasingly concerned about and affected by violence, growing social problems and lack of respect for each other and the world around them. Most parents of young children are searching for ways to help their offspring become self-confident and socially adept. Parents of teens often struggle with communication and relationships. Sometimes they do not know how to help when their children are confronting their own issues. They fear the influence of other teenagers and would like to stay an effective, positive force as their children navigate these difficult years.

Living Values: An Educational Program (LVEP) has produced this Facilitator Guide for Living Values Parent Groups in response to these concerns. It offers a forum for parents to share their wisdom and challenges, to explore their own values, and to increase their knowledge of sensible, practical and positive parenting skills.

Living Values Parent Groups, led by an experienced facilitator, provide a process through which to explore their own values and wishes for their children. The process-oriented sessions are designed so parents can:

- Assess which values are most important to them;
- Determine which values they want to impart to their children;
- Build awareness about how children learn about values; and

- Develop understanding and skills that parents can use in teaching values to their children.

Parents and caregivers will be asked to think, create and model the values they would like their children to enjoy. Additionally, methods are presented which show parents how to incorporate values as they nurture the development of their children. Living Values Parent Groups can be carried out as a precursor to Living Values Activities with the children—or as part of an existing parenting class or program.

Please note that throughout this guide the words "parents" and "caregivers" are used interchangeably.

# Duration of Parent Group Meetings

Living Values Parent Group meeting activities can be structured to meet the needs of parents and caregivers. For instance, there could be one orientation session and any number of sessions thereafter. At least ten sessions are suggested. This would allow parents to explore the values of peace, respect and love, and to learn nine Parenting Skills.

If an ongoing, supportive skills-building group is desired, weekly sessions of ninety minutes would be appropriate. If an introductory approach is used, an hour-long orientation meeting whenever the school or agency is beginning a new value unit would be appropriate.

# Using This Facilitator Guide

In addition to this Facilitator Guide for Living Values Parent Groups, each facilitator will need the Living Values Activities book appropriate for the ages of the children of the parents and caregivers participating.

All three sections included in this guide are designed for use by or consultation with a facilitator. Section 3 in particular (Parenting Skills) would require facilitation by someone knowledgeable in dealing with issues of childhood development.

## Section 1—The Group Process

The group process, as designed, sets the tone and flow of values-based workshops. A sample workshop describes a typical orientation session. Additionally, a Six-Step Framework for teaching values is included as a model for on-going sessions.

## Section 2—Parent Values Activities

This section provides values-based content to be used during the group process. The parent values activities complement and build upon the structured Living Values Activities for children and young adults. The values of focus are: Peace, Respect, Love, Happiness, Honesty, Humility, Responsibility, Simplicity, Tolerance, Cooperation, Freedom and Unity. Activities in this section are suggested for use:

- At Group Meetings—Activities are designed for the formal group process, with simulation and discussion a critical part of the learning. These activities acquaint the parents with the Living Values lessons their children may be doing in the classroom.
- At Home—Activities or suggestions are offered for parents or caregivers in the home setting.

Activities are offered on values-based behaviors for parents with children three years and above. However, many of the activities are adaptable for children two years of age. Additionally, since research has shown that children are able to learn even before being born, suggestions also are provided for that earliest stage of development. Parents with infants and one-year-olds would benefit by joining groups comprised of parents with toddlers.

## Section 3—Parenting Skills

This section addresses common parental concerns and offers specific skills to deal with those concerns. While parents can benefit from reading this material, it is more valuable as a facilitated group discussion. For facilitators who have not taught parenting classes, this section provides the type of issues which typically are raised by parents. Parenting Skills included are:

1. The Importance of Play and "Us Time"
2. Encouragement and Positively Building Behaviors
3. The Balance of Discipline and Love
4. Active Listening
5. Establishing a Ritual
6. Think Before Saying No
7. Time to Be
8. Staying Stable and Loving, and Communicating
9. "Time-Out" to Think and Communicate

From both a facilitator and participant standpoint, the ideal group would be comprised of parents with children of similar ages, since topics would be relevant for all participants.

# Facilitator Notes

This Facilitator Guide for Living Values Parent Groups provides sufficient information for facilitators to conduct values-based classes for parents and caregivers. It is recommended that a facilitator with experience leading parent groups attend a Living Values: An Educational Program training. Once that facilitator has done a couple of Living Values Parent Groups, he or she is likely to have sufficient knowledge about the program to share with other facilitators in their area. Small groups of facilitators may wish to meet and review the material, discussing questions and issues which may arise in a live workshop in their local areas. As facilitators gain more experience with this particular material, they are encouraged to network and share lessons learned throughout the process.

The role of facilitator or group leader is key to setting the tone of the workshops. Accepting group members and providing positive affirmations and respect are necessary to make group members feel they are in a safe environment. Giving regard and appreciation for all comments is important not only to create a rich learning environment but also to deepen the parents' acceptance of and value for the self. Especially in an adult learning environment, it is essential to draw upon the experience of the participants and to allow them to assimilate the material through their own learning styles and frames of reference. Knowledge of group dynamics and interactions among adults is a key aspect of facilitation.

Particularly with the Parenting Skills section, the facilitator needs to be sensitive to cultural issues and should offer only those Parenting Skills which are appropriate for the group, providing examples which are relevant to the culture. Introducing any of the Parenting Skills will undoubtedly raise issues and concerns and generate a good amount of group discussion. The facilitator should have an accurate balance between encouraging group members to share their views, opinions and experience and providing guidance and strategies for effective parenting.

As experienced group leaders know, participant sharing is invaluable to the learning process. As they share and listen, they recognize commonalties of each one's hopes, fears and challenges. The process-oriented approach of adult learning—as has been suggested here for each value—allows participants to learn that they already know many of the answers.

# Facilitators and Parents— Share with the World!

Facilitators and parents are warmly invited to share their experiences with Living Values: An Educational Program. You may share your activities and expertise with other facilitators and parents around the world through the Living Values Web site. Visit *www.livingvalues.net*. Or, send in your contribution to the nearest LVEP Country Coordinator.

**Annual Evaluation:** An important part of any program is evaluation. Your evaluation of the program and observations about changes with your children are very important. Kindly let the LVEP Coordinator in your country know you are using LVEP, and you will be sent an Educator Evaluation Form. Or, you may fill out this form on the web site.

We hope you enjoy Living Values. Thank you.

# SECTION ONE

# The Group Process

# ORIENTATION SESSION

Before the session, set up a list or posters of the values explored in Living Values: An Educational Program. A flip chart or board and some soft music will be needed.

## Introduction

The facilitator introduces himself or herself.

Ask parents or caregivers to introduce themselves. One way to do that is to ask participants to interview each other and then present their partner. You might ask them to share how many children they have, the children's ages, and one positive word they would use to describe their children.

**Introductory Activity:** You may wish to do one of the introductory activities from the *LVEP Educator Training Guide*. For example, "If I Were an Animal I Would Be a . . ." In this introductory activity participants are to think of one of their favorite animals, and the value or quality of that animal most important to them. Give each participant a sheet of blank paper with a straight pin at the top. Ask them to write the name of the animal (in big letters) on the top half of the paper and the value or quality of the animal on the bottom half. Explain that each person will be pinning his or her sheet of paper on the back of someone else, not letting that person see what is written.

In this introductory game, each participant introduces him or herself to another person, and then asks one question. The first task is to figure out the type of animal written on the paper pinned on their back. The one question must be able to be answered by a "yes" or "no." For example, "Does this animal have four legs?" "Is it a mammal?" Once they figure out the name of the animal, they are to try and figure out the virtue or quality.

Once the participants understand the directions, ask them to pin their sheet of paper on the back of someone else, not letting that person see what is written. Play some music as the game begins. Allow it to continue for ten to fifteen minutes, or until the noise begins to subside as people figure out the words on their back.

Variations: Ask them to put the names of famous champions of peace or justice or their heroes or heroines and the quality they admire. Or, ask each participant to write their favorite value at the top of a page, with a symbol representing it below. Then, play the same game as above.

# Background Information

If this is the first meeting of the group, the facilitator may wish to give some background information on Living Values: An Educational Program.

Living Values: An Educational Program (LVEP) is a values education program. It offers a variety of experiential values activities and practical methodologies to teachers and facilitators to enable children and young adults to explore and develop twelve key personal and social values: Peace, Respect, Love, Happiness, Honesty, Humility, Responsibility, Simplicity, Tolerance, Cooperation, Freedom and Unity. LVEP also contains special segments for use with parents and caregivers, as well as for refugees and children affected by war. As of March 2000, LVEP was already in use at over 1,800 sites in sixty-four countries.

Currently, there are six LVEP books:

*Living Values Activities for Children Ages 3–7*
*Living Values Activities for Children Ages 8–14*
*Living Values Activities for Young Adults*
*Living Values Parent Groups: A Facilitator Guide*
*LVEP Educator Training Guide*
*Living Values Activities for Refugees and Children-Affected-by-War*

LVEP is a partnership among educators around the world. It is its own non-profit entity. It is currently supported by UNESCO, sponsored by the Spanish Committee of UNICEF, the Planet Society, and the Brahma Kumaris, in consultation with the Education Cluster of UNICEF (New York).

The purpose of the Living Values Educational Program is to provide guiding principles and tools for the development of the whole person, recognizing that the individual is comprised of physical, intellectual, emotional and spiritual dimensions.

The aims of LVEP are:

- To help individuals think about and reflect on different values and the practical implications of expressing them in relation to themselves, others, the community and the world at large;
- To deepen understanding, motivation and responsibility with regard to making positive personal and social choices;
- To inspire individuals to choose their own personal, social, moral and spiritual values and to be aware of practical methods for developing and deepening them; and

- To encourage educators, parents and caregivers to look at education as providing students with a philosophy of living, thereby facilitating their overall growth, development and choices so they may integrate themselves into the community with respect, confidence, and purpose.

The Living Values Parent Groups are included as a critical part of this project because parents are the first and most important teachers of values.

Please refer to the Setting the Context section in any of LVEP's Living Values Activities for Children or Young Adults for more information.

# Reflections

To encourage each parent to reflect on the values that are important to them, play soft music and slowly speak the reflective passage below, allowing plenty of time for thought.

**Introductory Remark:** *"Values affect our lives every moment. They are a guiding force in all we do and pursue. When our values are in congruence with our actions, we are in harmony. But what are values? And how did we develop them? I would like you to reflect on some of your values as I ask you to think about several things. Please write down your responses."*

Play some relaxing music, and begin the following Reflective exercise. Allow the participants sufficient time to respond; while approximate pausing times are suggested, each group is different. Observe when they are finished.

- I would like you to think of a person who has influenced your life in a positive way. (Pause for a few moments.)
- What values or qualities did you see in that person that made a difference for you? Please write down the qualities or values that made him or her important to you. (Pause for a minute.)

- If everyone in the world had that quality, or demonstrated that value constantly, would the world be different? (Pause.)
- I would like you to think of the songs you love. What values are reflected through those words and music? Write those down. (Allow two or three minutes.)
- Think of poems, quotes, and books that are important to you. What qualities are within them? (Allow three or more minutes.)
- What images are important to you? Think of your favorite scenes, views or perhaps statues. What values and feelings are elicited by those? (Allow three or more minutes.)
- Remember a few especially positive moments of your life—what feelings did you experience then? What value did you demonstrate in those moments? (Allow four or more minutes.)
- Think of what you enjoy most about being a parent. What is it that you value within the moments you are remembering?

Ask the parents to form groups of three or four to share some of their experiences and values from this exercise. Allow ten to fifteen minutes.

- Now, I would like you to take five minutes to think about six values that are most important in your life. Please write them down. (Play reflective music softly.)

Ask participants to share. Have them call out their answers and write them on the flip chart. Summarize: *"It seems that we share many values."*

Say: *"A very interesting project was done several years ago called Global Cooperation for a Better World. In this project, thousands of small groups of people from all different cultures, religions, ages and socioeconomic status gathered in 129 countries to visualize a better world. They were asked to visualize how they would feel in a better world, how their relationships would be and what the environment would look like. Can you guess their responses?"* Ask:

- How would you like to feel inside?
- How would you like your relationships to be?
- What would you like the environment to be like?

*"It seems that not only do we want the same qualities in our relationships, but that human beings in all cultures share universal values. While we share universal values, we are not living the values we share. It is the premise of this program that if we did live our values, we would create a better world."*

- Let's explore for a few minutes how children develop values. I would like you to think back to a time when you were little, and remember those experiences when you learned what was important to you. (Play some music and allow them to reflect for a couple of minutes.)
- Now I'd like you to think about the very first value you can remember having—and how old you were.
- Would some of you like to share? (Write down their responses.)

Reflect on some of their responses as they fall into different categories, e.g., *"So, some of you learned to appreciate that value when . . ."*

---

FACILITATOR NOTE

While most of the people will probably mention positive experiences, some may mention negative experiences that showed them why a value was important, for example, when someone lied about them they learned the importance of honesty. Note their experience in a few words on the flip chart. You may want to question further to find out if at the time of the experience another person took the time to discuss honesty, or listened to them, etc.

---

The Group Process

• As children, what would you like to tell the adults of the world? What would you like them to do? How would you like them to treat you? Ask them to call out their responses, and record them on the flipchart as you repeat or paraphrase what they say.

*"I think you have just described a values-based atmosphere."*

---

FACILITATOR NOTE

Say this if they have just done that. Based on previous experience, the participants usually say such things as "listen to me; love me; respect me; let me play; give me limits," etc. If they have not described a values-based atmosphere, simply summarize what they have said.

---

State, *"Thank you. Now, I'd like you to use your imagination. Picture in your mind's eye your children—but they are all grown up. All your hopes for them are realized. What values do they have? Please write those down."* Allow several minutes to think and write.

*"Now, I want you to picture your children at their current ages. Imagine the values that you would like to see in your children and in your relationship with your children. (pause) What are your interactions like? (pause) How do you feel inside when values-based interactions are taking place? (share) What did you picture?" (share)*

Then ask the parents to form groups of three or four to share their experiences and thoughts with each other. Allow them ten minutes.

Ask each group to briefly report back to the whole group. Acknowledge the group's insights and contributions.

# Choosing the Values

You might ask the group what values they would like to explore, and make a list of those values as they share. The list of values almost always includes peace and respect. It is recommended that the group start with these two values.

There may be circumstances in which other values have already been chosen. For example, in some daycare centers, nursery schools or elementary and secondary schools, the administration or faculty may have already chosen values to focus on for the entire year. Or they may have chosen one value for each month. If that is the case, discuss the school values plan with the parents and ask if they would like to follow that sequence of values. It is of great benefit to have the school and home working on the same values at the same time. If, however, parents decide they want to start with a value that has not been chosen, listen, list their reasons and let them come to a consensus. They will be more motivated to be involved when they are part of the decision.

Conclude with thanks for their participation, a statement of how important their roles are as parents and caregivers, and a statement that you will look forward to seeing them next _____ to explore the value of _____.

---

# Six-Step Framework
# for Session 2 and Ongoing Sessions

## Step One: Discuss the Value

Take up the value the group has identified as its choice. You may wish to read a short, pertinent selection from *Living Values: A Guidebook.* Or you may wish to read a poem or a short story on the particular value. Ask, *"What does that value mean to you?"* (share) As they share, record an abbreviated form of their response on the board or flip chart.

## Step Two: Discuss How We Communicate That Value

Ask, *"So how do we communicate this value? How do we teach it to our children?* (share) *How do we increase the experience of _____ in the home? In our relationship with our children?* (share) *In our interactions with our children?* (share) *In the home environment?* (share) *In the self?"* (share) The parents are likely to say that children learn from the behaviors of parents. If they do not bring up that point, the facilitator may wish to do so, saying,

"Everything we do teaches values. The way we interact with others—what we say, how we say it, and what we do after saying it. If I were to lecture a twelve-year-old about honesty one day, read from a scripture the next day, read a story about honesty the following day, and then try to cheat on the price of a ticket to a fair the fourth day, the twelve-year-old would learn from my behavior that cheating is okay." Ask for comments.

## Step Three: Play with the Value

### *What Other Values Activities Can We Do at Home?*

The group may want to spend three sessions each on the values of Peace, Respect and Love as there are more values activities in these units. In the first session at which parents actually do some of the living values activities for children, present the information in The Importance of Play, Parenting Skill #1 in Section 3. One or two sessions may be sufficient for other values.

Refer to Parent Values Activities in Section 2 for the value the group is exploring that week. Section 2 has suggestions for parent activities, many of which are adapted from the Living Values Activities for Children books. Parents may wish to play with the exercises used at the age level of their children. That is really fun. Hopefully, the group will spend at least half its time playing and experimenting with the values.

The values activities for parents to do at home is a limited list. Parents are likely to have more suggestions of their own. Encourage them to share their ideas with others (you can even send them to us or post them on the Living Values Web site!). That will build enthusiasm and delight. This step is a perfect opportunity to have them share songs, games and wisdom from their heritage.

## Step Four: Discuss How Each Parent Can Implement at Home

### Present Parenting Skills as Appropriate

Open the discussion to their feelings, thoughts and obstacles to implementing the value in the home setting. Many parents have not had parenting classes, and some have had negative or abusive role models. Hence, this is a perfect time to listen carefully, open up the discussion to suggestions from other caregivers, and teach appropriate Parenting Skills for the situation. A facilitator who has taught parenting classes will be well prepared for these discussions, as often parents are receptive to input and in need of practical strategies to reduce conflict and stress.

To aid facilitators with less extensive parent-group experience, Section 3 contains Parenting Skills in response to common parental concerns as well as information addressing those concerns. The facilitator may wish to include one Parenting Skill in each session for the first nine sessions. Present them in order, for example, doing Parenting Skill 1, The Importance of Play and "Us Time" in the first session.

Of course, the facilitator needs to be sensitive to the needs of the group and should feel free to present Parenting Skills as the need arises. The facilitator also needs to be sensitive to cultural issues and should offer only those Parenting Skills which are appropriate and pertinent to the group, tailoring examples as necessary.

## Step Five: Adjourn with Homework

End the session with an (optional) activity or good wishes to enjoy their values activities with the children.

## Step Six: Next Session

### What Worked?

At the following session, ask participants to share their experiences/successes at home. Ask, *"What worked and what did not?"* (share) *"What changes did they notice?"* (share) Listen, enjoy the stories, acknowledge and congratulate them on their efforts. If the group wants to continue with that value, play a couple more activities from that value exercise. The group may choose to open each session with one of the peace visualizations.

When you are ready to take up the next value, start with Step One again, discussing that value in the formal group setting.

# SECTION TWO

## Parent Values Activities

# FOR PARENTS

## For Parents of Infants and Toddlers

A peaceful, loving attitude is a special gift for children from the time they are in the womb. Some parents are aware of the child's ability to absorb while in the womb, and they start teaching before the child is born by talking or reading aloud to the child or playing music. Research has shown that infants recognize the voices of people who had been talking to them; infants also had relaxed responses to the music they had heard while in the womb.

It is said that mothers can distinguish the different personalities of their children displayed even within the womb, and that each child knows whether he or she is wanted. In this light, parents are encouraged to think of the embryo as a conscious being with an ability to absorb love and peace.

Once born, there is constant interplay between the child and the caregivers. The infant needs to be touched, held, nurtured, cooed at and tended to in a consistent, loving, and patient manner. The bonding between the parent and child is essential not only for a good relationship, but also for the lifelong well-being of the child.

Infants and toddlers are especially responsive to the attitude and emotions of their primary caregivers. They respond in a healthy way emotionally and physically to loving care, and poorly to irritation and peacelessness on the part of the caregiver. They become distressed when the parent is grieving, depressed or angry, and they are more stable when the parent is unhurried and happy.

Simply knowing the importance of the quality of what we give to an infant allows more attention to that process. Filling the self with contentment, peace and love allows the baby to experience more of those qualities. (Parenting Skill 7, Time to Be, in Section 3, covers this point in more depth.)

Parents and caregivers are encouraged to consider the following values activities as the parent/child relationship develops:

- Play with the baby, and treat the child as an individual. Make time to play with your child daily. Enjoy the child, and yourself.
- Play peaceful and happy music that naturally creates the emotions you want the baby to experience.
- Tell the baby nursery tales and rhymes.
- Use the words "peaceful," "loving," "cooperative," "content," "sweet," and "happy" with your baby and toddler. Label your own positive feelings for them when you are experiencing those emotions.
- Do not *only* comment on physical appearance, such as telling the child, *"You are cute,"* or *"What a darling outfit."*
- Verbalize their positive qualities and ways of being. Notice when they are being gentle with a toy or a pet.
- Choose safe, peace-giving toys—toys that are fun and allow the infant or toddler to experience his or her own creativity.
- Play peek-a-boo with puppets. Have the puppets give lots of love, too. Enjoy a few quiet, peaceful moments with a star puppet, with God or with an angel.
- Choose videos and cartoons carefully. Most cartoons are not suitable for children under three—they are violent. In the parent groups, caregivers can share which programs have friendly cartoon characters, and funny,

nurturing characters. Limit the time in front of the television to one hour a day. More than four hours a day limits a child's development in several ways.

- Do not expose the infant to hearing violence on television, radio or within the community, or to arguments and fighting of parents. Be aware of the child when older siblings or adults are watching movies. Is the child being exposed to images, noises and words too grown-up for his or her age? Be aware of the impact of the environment. A child under the age of three can not place events in time and space, but does record the emotional impact of events.

- If the baby has an older brother or sister who is also quite young, be careful to give attention to that child as well. Parents might post a note on the front door when guests are coming to see the baby. Ask guests to notice and attend to the older sibling first. As parents, involve the older sibling in holding the baby and helping with small tasks. Give older siblings eye contact and chat with them at least half the time when you and they are with the infant.

## Can I Use the Living Values Activities with Two-Year-Olds?

Yes. Facilitators, parents, and caregivers can easily use many of the activities in *Living Values Activities for Children Ages 3–7* with two-year-olds. Simplify the language, give a little more help and they respond wonderfully.

# PEACE

## For Parents of Two- Through Seven-Year-Olds

### At Group Meetings

- Review the Peace Points in *Living Values Activities for Children Ages 3–7,* so parents can hear how peace is explained to children that age.

- Continue with the Imagining a Peaceful World exercise.

- Present The Importance of Play and "Us Time," Parenting Skill 1, in Section 3 during the first session on the value of peace. Ask parents to share their experiences playing with their children the next session. Ask, *"How is it going? Are you enjoying it? How are you finding ways to make time? Is it easy to get into the spirit of play? Do you notice any changes?"* Proceed with one Parenting Skill presentation and discussion at each session.

- Make and play with Peace Finger Puppets. (See *Living Values Activities for Children Ages 3–7.*)

- Have one parent read "The Star Story" (*Living Values Activities for Children Ages 3–7,* Appendix) during the group session. (At home, they can follow up on this story with the children at nap time or when tucking them in at night.) Do the Peace Star exercise.

- Review Arms Are for Hugging (*Living Values Activities for Children Ages 3–7*) and teach the conflict resolution skills. Have the parents pretend to be children and take turns resolving conflicts as the parent.

- Parents may have a favorite peace song they sang as a child. Sing it for the group.

## At Home

When children bring home their Peace Finger Puppets, parents may wish both to admire and to talk to the Peace Puppets. Perhaps the Peace Finger Puppets could come out and play when there is a conflict at home—they might have some good ideas.

- Set up a Peace Corner. It could be in a corner in the bedroom of the house, and a bed sheet could be used to create a tent. You could decorate it together, using pictures of whatever makes you feel peaceful or gives a warm feeling inside. The Peace Corner could be used for peace visualizations before nap time or to sit together with little ones and sing a song and play. Perhaps the Peace Finger Puppets could live there, too. This could be a place to resolve conflicts when the children are quarreling.
- Sing peace songs together while you do things. Sing as you take a walk or swing in a swing.
- Let the children know when they are "making peace." Give them a peace prize of a kiss or a hug.
- When you make cookies, tortillas, or chappatis, roll some out so you and the children can make peace symbols with it. Examples are: doves, peace signs or whatever your imagination warrants.
- Include peace in your prayers with the children.

# For Parents of Children Eight Years and Older

## At Group Meetings

- Review Peace Reflection Points from *Living Values Activities for Children Ages 8–14* and practice visualizing a peaceful world.

- If group members are comfortable with each other, the facilitator can ask them to sing their favorite peace songs. Whoever knows the song can join in.
- Present one Parenting Skill from Section 3 at each session, beginning with The Importance of Play and "Us Time," Parenting Skill 1. Proceed with one Parenting Skill presentation and discussion at each session.
- Show parents the peace unit activities in *Living Values Activities for Children Ages 8–14.* Look at Time Capsule and A World of Peace Versus a World of Conflict. Do those activities with parents if they wish.
- Form a circle. Go around the circle, asking parents to complete the sentence, "I feel most peaceful when . . ." Then ask them to complete the sentence, "I think my daughter (or son) might feel most peaceful when . . ." Continue to go around the circle until they have said something about each one of their children.
- Review Conflict Resolution and Arms Are for Hugging lessons. Have the parents pretend to be children and take turns resolving conflicts as the parent.

## At Home

- Play peace songs your children like. Sing peace songs together—perhaps as you walk or ride.
- Let your children know when you appreciate their being a "giver of peace" or a "river of peace." Acknowledge their positive efforts toward communication during a conflict resolution session in which they may have been involved.
- Share your feelings about peace with your children, making your comments appropriate to their age.

- Invite them into the kitchen. Make peace symbols together out of bread or cookie dough, or decorate a cake with peace symbols. Perhaps they can do this with friends.

- Both caregivers and children can take turns in the evening selecting favorite peace points from their culture, religion or belief system. They could present peace points for one minute before dinner or some other time in your daily routine.

- Ask your teenager to share his or her peace visualization. Listen intently.

- Discuss violent movies with your spouse. Are you, as adults, able to give these up? If yes, discuss whether you want to limit your children's access to these at home. If you are unsure, observe the mood of your children after they watch the next three violent movies. Observe your own thoughts and mood after watching a violent movie versus a peaceful, humanizing movie. Discuss with your spouse again. If you agree to renounce violent movies, talk to your children and share that decision with them. Let them know, *"Whatever we watch, we have those emotions running through our minds. There is no benefit in violent emotions going through our minds if we want to help create a peaceful world."* If you decide to implement this policy at home, stick to it. The protest won't last long. If older teenagers choose to see violent movies with their peers outside the home, stay detached and content and listen to their experience.

- Ask your children what inspires them about peace. Listen to what they say.

- Visit a place where peace can be seen in action—perhaps a museum about a peace visionary, a center for non-violence or perhaps a shelter where they care for people.

- Ask yourselves, *"When do we feel most peaceful?"* Help each other create more of those moments.

# RESPECT

## For Parents of Two- Through Seven-Year-Olds

### At Group Meetings

- Review Respect Points in *Living Values Activities for Children Ages 3–7* so parents can hear how respect is explained to children that age.
- Present Encouragement and Positively Building Behaviors, Parenting Skill 2, in Section 3, if it has not been done previously. Ask parents to list the qualities they love about their child and to think of specific praise for a quality they notice in a couple of behaviors.
- Sing or listen to "Each One of Us Is Beautiful." (*Living Values Activities for Children Ages 3–7*). (This is fun to sing with your children when on your way to the market.) Ask parents to share songs that make them feel wonderful inside.
- Review Active Listening, Parenting Skill 4, in Section 3. Ask them to practice active listening in small groups of three. One person is the talker, another the active listener, and the third the observer. The three should take turns with each role.

  —For the first round, talkers share something positive that happened to them.

  —For the second round, talkers share something that made them feel sad or mad.

  —For the third round, talkers pretend to be their child and share something they were concerned about recently.

—After each round, the group of three should provide feedback to each other on demonstrated active listening skills through sharing of observations and experiences.

- For homework during the week, ask parents and caregivers to actively listen if a child has a problem he or she feels badly about.

## At Home

- Parents may wish to play My Hands (*Living Values Activities for Children Ages 3–7*). But, instead of putting down one good action that the child's hands do (as the teacher did at school), the parent can help the child list many good actions. Do that with all the young ones, if you have more than one child, and make up a simple song to go with the activity. Have fun changing the song as your activities change!

- Put up on the wall your child's Me Silhouette (*Living Values Activities for Children Ages 3–7*). When your child brings the artwork home, enjoy how he or she shows it to you. As you happily describe it, watch your child's face light up.

- Use specific praise with the child several times a day, naming the quality which was demonstrated.

- Give your children full attention and listen to them for at least a few minutes a day. That is one of the best ways for you to show respect and for them to feel valued.

- Occasionally thank your children for listening well.

- Stay content when you help them with their homework. If you start to get frustrated, leave for a few minutes and have a cup of tea. Detach. With your patience, they'll catch on a lot faster. Make only positive comments while they are doing their homework. Model how to do a problem in the homework when they do not know how, then help them do

a couple. Ask them to call you when they've done one problem independently. Say, *"Wow, you did that one all by yourself . . . Okay, do some
more—then call me if you like."*

- If the child is speaking in a demanding or disrespectful tone of voice, you
  may wish to say, *"How would* _____ *say that?"*
  (Insert the name of one of the child's favorite peaceful cartoon characters
  or heroes.) Then praise the new tone of voice with a smile and say,
  *"That's a tone of voice I like to hear."*

# For Parents of Children Eight Years and Older

## At Group Meetings

- After the facilitator has reviewed Respect Reflection Points from *Living
  Values Activities for Children Ages 8–14*, discuss the points and answer the
  same questions listed in the children's section.
- Review exercises the students will be doing: Me Mobiles and Colors of
  Respect and Disrespect *(Living Values Activities for Children Ages 8–14)*.
- Do My Qualities *(Living Values Activities for Children Ages 8–14)* with parents. Give each parent a piece of paper. Each parent is to write their
  name at the top of the paper and pass it around the circle. Every other
  caregiver writes down the qualities they see in the person whose name
  appears at the top.
- Ask parents to share their favorite stories about self-respect. Include
  stories from every culture in the area, if possible.
- Present Encouragement and Positively Building Behaviors, Parenting Skill
  2, in Section 3, if it has not been done previously. Ask parents to list the
  qualities they love about their child and to think of one quality they

would like to see bloom in that child. In groups of three, practice giving specific praise and naming the quality demonstrated.

- Review Active Listening, Parenting Skill 4, in Section 3. Ask parents to practice active listening in small groups of three. (Please see the section— For Parents of Two- Through Seven-Year-Olds—for examples to use when practicing.)

- For homework during the week, ask parents to actively listen to each of their children.

- Suggest they listen to teenagers without adding their own view or reacting negatively. Practice for one week. Discuss what happened the following week.

## At Home

- Use specific praise with children, positively affirming behaviors and qualities.

- Give your children full attention and listen to them at least a few minutes a day. That is one of the best ways for you to show respect and for them to feel valued.

- Share stories about self-respect—perhaps new ones you heard in the parent group. Afterward, find time to discuss with each child the qualities you see in him or her.

- Stay content when you help them with homework. If you start to get frustrated, leave for a few minutes and have a cup of tea. Detach. With your patience, they'll catch on a lot faster. Make only positive comments when they do homework. If they make an error, simply go over it with them once. Be interested in their questions. If you do not know the answer, help them investigate. Know the most important thing you are teaching is an attitude toward learning.

- If your child's attitude becomes disrespectful, find time to sit down for a chat. Let the child know you noticed his or her attitude, and you know when there is disrespect on the outside, it is often a reflection of disrespect on the inside. Ask what is happening, and listen. Affirm the child's good qualities and efforts at the end of the conversation.
- Give them hugs and positive remarks about what you treasure about them—for no reason at all!

# LOVE

## For Parents of Two- Through Seven-Year-Olds

### At Group Meetings

- Review Love Points in *Living Values Activities for Children Ages 3–7* so parents can hear how love is explained to children that age.
- Do the Quietly Being exercise, Filling Up With Love (*Living Values Activities for Children Ages 3–7*).
- Ask parents to share with other parents their favorite stories about love. Stories may be legends from their different cultural backgrounds or from books they read as children. The parents may want to exchange books so they can take turns reading to their children at home.
- Continue to present the Parenting Skills in Section 3 that have not been reviewed. After reviewing Establishing a Ritual, Parenting Skill 5, discuss: Part of love is creating the feeling of being safe. Ask the parents to share rituals their parents did, and rituals they enjoy at home.

- The parents may want to do the Hearts activity (*Living Values Activities for Children Ages 3–7*). Ask them to share how they feel when they feel big-hearted and to explain what allows them to stay in that place. Ask, *"What helps us when we are sad-hearted?"* Discuss.
- As a group, sing a song from *Living Values Activities for Children Ages 3–7*, or another song from your culture. At home, parents may wish to sing this when playing with the children or when dancing or making something for someone.

## At Home

- Parents may want to share with their children their own version of the Quietly Being exercise Filling Up With Love, as the children go to sleep at night. Parents may wish to add ideas from their own faith or of the image of the child being wrapped in a cocoon of the caregivers' love.
- Love is sharing. Sharing is often difficult for toddlers, but it can be easier to learn if there is plenty of what they are sharing rather than only one. Before the child has a playmate over, express that there are plenty of cookies, chocolates or sweets to share with his or her friend. Encourage the child to offer it himself or herself to the playmate. Deliver praise with a smile. Say, *"You shared the chocolates; that was loving."*
- When a child does something special or is making an effort to learn a new skill, the parent may want to leave a little heart on the child's pillow or in a place that is "theirs." It could be a heart face with a happy smile or a heart shape with a couple of sweet words inside. Or, it could just be a heart note saying *"I love you."*
- Think about the routines and rituals you have at home. Would you like to add anything or change something? If there are two caretakers, are both participating in this special time?

- Parents could suggest the child write a note to or draw a picture for the grandparents or someone special in their lives. Tell the child, *"This is one way we can show our love."*
- It is always interesting to ask children how many hugs they need a day. A hug at the beginning of the day is a nice wake-up call.

# For Parents of Children Eight Years and Older

## At Group Meetings

- After the facilitator has reviewed Love Reflection Points in *Living Values Activities for Children Ages 8–14,* do the World of Love imagining activity.
- As a group, sing songs of love. Ask parents to share favorite songs when they were young. Learn songs from different cultures.
- Share the Words of the Heart activity (*Living Values Activities for Children Ages 8–14*) and provide the materials for parents to make a heart for each of their children. Enjoy cutting and pasting as you chat. Ask, *"How do you feel when you are big-hearted? What allows you to stay in that place? What helps when you are sad-hearted?"*
- Ask group members to share what their own parents said which made them feel loved. Ask, *"Does anybody want to share what made them not feel loved?"*
- Review Establishing a Ritual, Parenting Skill 5, in Section 3. Part of love is creating the feeling of being safe. When teenagers revert to playing with something they have not played with for years, it is sometimes because they feel a need for reassurance. This is a good time to do an old ritual with them.

- Review The Balance of Discipline and Love, Parenting Skill 5, in Section 3. In groups of three, practice explaining things to the "children" with this balance. Listen to how the "child" responds. Use active listening skills by repeating the essence of what was said. Explain and answer questions with love.

## At Home

- Parents may want to share with children ages eight through ten their own version of the imagining exercise, A World of Love, as they go to sleep at night. Parents may wish to add ideas from their own faith and of the image of the child being wrapped in a cocoon of love. While you could do this with the child when involved in the unit, if the child really likes it, you may wish to continue imagining one night a week or so. For older children, share with them that your homework from the parenting group on values is to do A World of Love imagining exercise with them every day for a week. Suggest you take turns doing it.

- Ask your children to help you find songs about universal love, love for humanity or love for nature.

- Love is sharing, caring, being a trustworthy friend. Positively affirm your children when they are exhibiting loving behaviors.

- Occasionally leave a sweet note for your child for no reason at all, or share something you appreciate about him or her. These notes are especially important when the child is struggling with the self, peers or the world.

- Think about the routines and rituals you have at home. Would you like to add anything or change something? If there are two caretakers, are both participating? Is there a time daily to share or a time weekly to do something together?

- Listen to your children's concerns and help them find practical ways to make the situation more positive. Keep your ears open for interesting, age-appropriate volunteer opportunities for children—ones which show them they can make a difference.
- At least one hug a day is still nice, no matter how old the person.

# HAPPINESS

## For Parents of Two- Through Seven-Year-Olds

### At Group Meetings

- Review Happiness Points in *Living Values Activities for Children Ages 3–7* so parents can hear how happiness is explained to children that age.
- Ask parents to share with the group what about their children makes them happy.
- Lead the parents in the Using Our Imagination exercise (*Living Values Activities for Children Ages 3–7*).
- Play children's games in the parent group. Ask the parents to tell about games they enjoyed as children. Play those.
- Look at Words Can Be Like Flowers or Thorns (*Living Values Activities for Children Ages 3–7*). If Encouragement and Positively Building Behaviors, Parenting Skill 2, in Section 3, has not been presented, do so. If it has, check with parents and ask how their skill is developing. Ask, *"Have you noticed any changes?"*
- Sing "The Happy Stars" song with the parent group. Ask parents to share any happy songs they know. Perhaps they would like to teach a couple to the group.

- As a group, review the Good Wishes section (*Living Values Activities for Children Ages 3–7*). Discuss how they can help their children have good wishes for others when others are feeling sad or bad.

## At Home

- Play games with your children at home or at the park. Enjoy being spontaneous and humorous occasionally.
- Little ones enjoy parents giving lots of hugs and physical contact during playtime. Your laughter is another wonderful gift.
- Caregivers might share with the children that giving good wishes is a way of giving happiness. Suggest, *"Let's send good wishes to _____ together."*
- Take a happy hike. Look at how the trees or the birds are happy.
- Sing "The Happy Stars" song with your children. Sing songs that give you a happy feeling. With your toddlers, do dancing exercises to the music.
- Have fun telling children's jokes when you have "Us Time." Listen and enjoy their jokes.
- Make a "Happy Thoughts" box. Everyone in the family can contribute thoughts, and each thought can be written on a slip of paper. Or, a tiny drawing can express a thought. The parent may want to do this as part of the evening ritual when you chat about the day, or it could be done at another time. A mother might write, *"I love Nick."* Other examples: *"Nick has a beautiful smile." "Hossein is sweet with his sister."* Avoid materialistic sentences. Encourage children to come up with a happy thought that has self- or interactive appreciation. Examples are: *"I like to make flower pictures." "I love playing with Daddy." "I am happy when I feel sweet inside."* Or, *"I love hugging the kitty cat."*
- Tell your children when you are proud of them.

# For Parents of Children Eight Years and Older

## At Group Meetings

- After the parents have discussed Happiness Reflection Points in *Living Values Activities for Children Ages 8–14,* play some favorite games from their own children's age group.
- Ask parents to answer questions listed in What Makes Happiness? (*Living Values Activities for Children Ages 8–14*).
- Review Talking to Myself (*Living Values Activities for Children Ages 8–14*) with the parents. Ask them to share about their own self-talk. Let them know how we talk to ourselves is often how we talk to others. If we get angry at ourselves internally, we usually get angry with others quickly. Most people have a "critical parent" inside and would benefit by developing a more understanding, supportive "gentle parent" inside. Form a circle and have each parent offer one "gentle parent" comment. If some find this difficult, suggest others help. Ask them to jot down things they say to themselves over the next week, and to write down what they can say instead. Enjoy each other's sharing when they report back at the next meeting.
- Ask one of the parents to read aloud the "Unicorns" story (*Living Values Activities for Children Ages 8–14*). Suggest parents might be interested in learning the secret of happiness their children created from that story.

## At Home

- Play a happy game with your children at least every other day. Enjoy being humorous sometimes.
- Relax a few minutes before the older kids come home so you can be fresh and feel delighted to see them.

Parent Values Activities

- Caregivers could share with children that giving good wishes is a way of giving happiness. When someone is having a hard time or when you hear news of violence, say, *"Let's send good wishes to* _____ *together."*
- Talk with your children about what makes happiness. Ask them, *"What do you think? What was the secret in the 'Unicorns' story?"* For a couple of weeks, everyone can think about and share what gives happiness. Focus on inner happiness and happiness in relationships as opposed to materialism. Find a relaxing time each day for the family to share—perhaps during a meal or after dinner. Write down the thoughts. Then, do some of the fun suggestions that result.
- Tell your children when you are proud of them.

# HONESTY

## For Parents of Two- Through Seven-Year-Olds

### At Group Meetings

- Review Honesty Points in *Living Values Activities for Children Ages 3–7* so parents can hear how honesty is explained to children that age.
- Read "The Emperor and the Flower Seeds" (*Living Values Activities for Children Ages 3–7,* Appendix). Discuss. Ask parents to share their favorite stories of honesty. Perhaps they know a legend, or they can bring a favorite children's story to the next parent meeting.
- Always keep your promises. When you say "yes," stick to it; and when you say "no," stick to that, too. Review Think Before You Say No, Parenting Skill 6, in Section 3.

- Tell your children the truth. Make it simple and kind, but let them know what is happening when there are changes about which they need to know. Discuss.

## At Home

- When appropriate, let your children know you appreciate their honesty.
- When you detect that a very young child is telling you less than the truth, gently tell him or her that this is not story time or pretend time, you want to know what really happened. *"Please tell me again, step by step, what happened."* For very little ones, only question once, and then let it go.
- If a child older than four years has been caught telling lies, do not question him or her about the events. That may have the negative consequence of increasing the lies. Try to figure out what happened without questioning him or her, and then say, *"_____ happened, and so your consequence is _____."* Provide a small, logical consequence. Then, on another day, ask this child to tell you about something you know happened, and praise his or her honesty. Say, *"You told me what really happened. That was honesty. I like that."*
- Tell your children stories about the courage to be honest as part of your bedtime ritual.
- Think before you say "yes" or "no," and stick to it. Set boundaries for their behavior and keep to them. Be consistent.

# For Parents of Children Eight Years and Older

## At Group Meetings

- Discuss the Honesty Reflection Points from *Living Values Activities for Children Ages 8–14.*

Parent Values Activities

- Read "The Emperor and the Flower Seeds" (*Living Values Activities for Children Ages 8–14*, Appendix). Discuss. Perhaps parents know a legend about honesty they would like to tell.
- Discuss some of the questions under One Minute of Courage (*Living Values Activities for Children Ages 8–14*). Discuss the effects of cheating on society. Ask them to share why they feel honesty is important in the home.
- Discuss the importance of always keeping your promises. Ask, *"How did you feel as children when promises were broken?"* Discuss: What were they glad that their own parents said "no" to? Do they wish they had said "no" on some issues and "yes" on others?

## At Home

- When appropriate, let your children know you appreciate their honesty.
- When you detect your child is not telling the truth, tell him or her the truth is important to you. Say, *"Where there is love and truth, honesty should naturally exist. I would like you to tell me the whole truth. I know that it can be hard and can take a lot of courage, but I promise to listen."* After giving that loving but real message, detach and leave. If your child has done something "bad" which has gotten him or her in trouble, listen rather than get mad. If you get mad and beat them when they are in trouble at age twelve, they will not come to you if there is bigger trouble later on. Listening allows trust to bloom.
- When a child has lied, do not question him or her about the particular event, as the child might lie again. Try to figure out what happened, and then say, *"_____ happened, and so your consequence is _____."* Provide a small, logical consequence. On another day, ask the child to tell you about things you

*Parent Values Activities*

know happened, and praise his or her honesty. Say, *"I appreciate your telling me the truth."* Build up these experiences.

- Tell your children the truth. Make it kind and appropriate to their age level, but let them know what is happening when there are changes about which they need to know.
- Point out the importance of honesty and the negative consequences of deceit. Point out why you do some of the things you do, as appropriate. For example, why you pay a worker a living wage rather than the minimum wage, why it is important to tell the person at the counter when they give back too much change, etc.

# HUMILITY

# For Parents of Two- Through Seven-Year-Olds

## At Group Meetings

- Review Humility Points in *Living Values Activities for Children Ages 3–7* so parents can hear how humility is explained to children that age.
- Have parents play the Humble Cartoon Characters exercise (*Living Values Activities for Children Ages 3–7*).
- Sing "My Wings." Have the parents think of songs that give the feeling of greatness and peace, that is, greatness and humility within. Sing them with the group.
- Share stories of greatness and humility. Tell your favorites.

## At Home

- Praise your child for listening, sharing and patiently awaiting his or her turn.

- If the child is speaking in a bragging tone of voice, you may wish to say, *"How would _____ say that?"* (Insert the name of one of the child's favorite peaceful cartoon characters or heroes who speaks with a confident but not a bragging tone of voice.) Then praise the new tone of voice with a smile and say, *"That's a tone of voice I like to hear."*

- Praise your child for not reacting, but staying full of self-respect and power, even when someone is slightly uncomplimentary or calls him or her a name.

# For Parents of Children Eight Years and Older

## At Group Meetings

- Review and discuss the Humility Reflection Points from *Living Values Activities for Children Ages 8–14.*

- Ask parents to do the Heroes Have Humility exercise (*Living Values Activities for Children Ages 8–14*).

- Ask parents to think of songs that give the feeling of greatness and peace, that is, greatness and humility, within. Sing them within the group. (Sing them at home.)

- Ask parents to share favorite stories of humility and greatness. Ask, *"Who do you remember who had that balance—friends, relatives, movie stars, politicians?"* (Find the right moment to share one with the children.)

## At Home

- Continue to affirm your children's good qualities. Offer short, matter-of-fact, appreciative comments when they are generous with a sibling, share or let go of something they were holding too tightly.

- When they ask you if something is good and you know they know it is—and they know why it is good because they have been receiving specific praise—look at them with the look and emotion that it is truly well done, and say: *"You tell me what you think."* That will help them develop the ability to give self-praise and have intrinsic motivation.

- When they are bragging, grin and ask: *"Hey, may I hear that again, but in your self-respect-and-humility tone?"* When their response is without arrogance, say, *"Thanks,"* and give them a smile. Or, when they are bragging, insert the name of one of their favorite peace heroes and ask if you can hear that comment again with _____'s tone.

- Listen when their feelings are hurt or when they feel unappreciated when someone does not thank them for all their work. Quietly let them know, *"God always knows, and you always know. Feel good inside because you did what was right. Hooray for you."*

- Tell your children, *"Good for you"* when they maintain self-respect when someone is uncomplimentary or calls them a name. Help them generate self-respecting, assertive responses, as appropriate. Positively affirm that only those with self-respect can create peace, and that he or she is such a one.

# RESPONSIBILITY

## For Parents of Two- Through Seven-Year-Olds

### At Group Meetings

- Review Responsibility Points in the *Living Values Activities for Children Ages 3–7* so parents can hear how different aspects of responsibility are explained to children that age.
- Discuss experiences. Ask, *"Do you remember when you were little and started to do things? What made you feel proud of yourself? When have your children gleamed with pride? What attitude is most productive in helping children take pride in their achievements?"*

### At Home

- Allow your little ones to help you with easy household chores. Have fun showing them how to do things. Set aside twenty minutes when everyone helps "make our house shine." Allow them to stir food in the kitchen, wipe something down, sweep, help set the table, etc. Make sure you assign something at which they will be successful. Note their activity, and praise them for being so helpful or such a good helper.
- Notice when your child is being fair, and affirm that positive action.
- Notice when your child is making an effort at a new self-care skill and praise him or her. At times this requires allowing them to do something alone and prompting and praising, rather than more quickly doing it yourself. Verbalize what they did and that they're being responsible, taking care of themselves.

*Parent Values Activities*

- Set up age-appropriate regular chores or responsibilities for the children. Monitor initially so they begin to feel proud of themselves as you watch them accomplishing the task. After a while, decrease praise for doing the task and praise them for remembering and taking responsibility for the task.

# For Parents of Children Eight Years and Older

## At Group Meetings

- Discuss Responsibility Reflection Points from *Living Values Activities for Children Ages 8–14*.
- Review the children's activities in the Responsibility section.
- Discuss experiences. Ask, *"Do you remember when you were little and started to do things? What made you feel proud of yourself? When you were older, what did you like to hear? What attitudes have you found most productive in helping your own children take pride in their achievements?"*

## At Home

- Notice when your child is being fair. Notice when your child is taking care of another. Affirm children's positive actions and let them know you appreciate their being responsible and loving.
- When a new situation or problem is arising for your child, ask, *"What do you think?"* Compliment him or her for thinking it through and coming up with some alternatives.
- If there is currently a lack of cooperation with chores, have a family meeting. Make a plan. Perhaps have a time during the day when everyone helps for twenty or thirty minutes. Set a buzzer and off you all go! Or

make a list of the chores that need doing. Ask for volunteers among the children, or divide the chores yourself among the children, depending on the situation. Post the list on a wall. Positively notice their helping actions, or give them a smile. Do not nag. After three days, review the chores list together and ask for difficulties or suggestions. Positively remark on the improvement, and come up with ideas to deal with the remaining obstacles. After that, weekly family meetings are an ideal time to keep up the momentum and positivity for helping with chores (and for meeting about many other things as well!).

- Notice when your child is making an effort to try a new skill, and praise him or her. At times that requires allowing the child to do something alone rather than more quickly doing it yourself. Praise what the child has done correctly, and show him or her how to correct the areas for improvement.

- When they want a new freedom, think about it. Once you have sincerely considered both the positive and negative consequences and discussed it with the other parent if applicable, sit down and discuss that freedom with your child. Ask, *"With that additional right, what do you think the responsibilities should be?"* Compliment him or her for thinking it through, if appropriate. If you, as a parent, are uncomfortable with allowing that freedom, think about why that is so and clearly present your reasons to the child.

- When they want to do something for which you think they are not prepared—yet they are old enough to do it—ask them what they think they will need. Respectfully guide them to discover what in reality that new idea will require. Give them your vote of confidence, your good wishes and let them go with love. In the future, they will more frequently turn to you for guidance.

# SIMPLICITY

## For Parents of Two- Through Seven-Year-Olds

### At Group Meetings

- Review Simplicity Points in *Living Values Activities for Children Ages 3–7* so parents can hear how simplicity can be explained to children that age.
- Review activities in the children's section. Do one of the activities. Ask parents to share their favorite simple things to play with as a child.
- Share stories of the traditions in your different cultures.
- Suggest parents take a nature walk together. Discuss conservation. Share practical suggestions and new ideas about conservation.

### At Home

- Allow your children to use things in the house to play creatively. Chairs and blankets make great indoor tents.
- Recycle things for play. For instance, an old inner tube from a large truck or tractor is great for back yard play—to bounce on and roll around in. Containers from a fruit or vegetable stand can become trains, or whatever else you dream up. Let the children play in piles of fallen leaves, or make a special play place outside. Have a box for discarded household items— "treasures" they can use in imaginary games.
- Recycle things in the house. Set up a place in your home where paper is recycled. They can use that to draw and fold.
- Enjoy making things yourself. Stringing together popcorn for the Christmas tree is a simple but fun tradition in some countries. In other

countries, a decoration of colored paper which has been folded, shaped and strung together is used for festivals.

- Be simple, natural and economical. In the kitchen, ask the children to help you stir in nuts to make porridge or granola that is one-half the price of advertised cereals.

- Take nature walks with the children. Enjoy the beauty of the trees or of whatever form of nature is around you. Think about and share lessons nature offers us.

- Honor the earth in simple ways. Teach your children not to be litter bugs. Never throw litter or rubbish on the ground, but place it in a garbage can or rubbish bin, or carry it back with you so it can be disposed of properly. Explain why we make the extra effort not to litter.

- Let your children know their smiles are beautiful. Let your children know that their smiles give joy to others.

- Think of little rhymes together about simplicity and the beauty of nature.

# For Parents of Children Eight Years and Older

## At Group Meetings

- Review and discuss Simplicity Reflection Points from the *Living Values Activities for Children Ages 8–14*.

- Suggest parents take a nature walk together. (Perhaps the group could meet in a park that week.) Follow the suggestions for A Nature Walk (*Living Values Activities for Children Ages 8–14*), including spending fifteen minutes in silence.

- Next week, do a simple art project together, and share stories of the traditions in your different cultures.

- Review the activities in the children's section on conservation and respect for the earth.
- The parents may want to discuss conservation and practical ways they can conserve at home. Share traditions, stories and methods of simplicity from different cultures.
- Review Simplicity Is Being Natural, Simplicity Is Beautiful (*Living Values Activities for Children Ages 8–14*). Discuss the messages you receive from different sources, including advertisements. What are the messages of many advertisements aimed at children? Take several of the messages the group perceives from the mass media as a whole, and think of what would be a more timeless message in response—from the viewpoint of the natural beauty of the self and of nature.

## At Home

- Listen to your child's ideas on conservation, and decide what you would like to do as a family. Think about what you can recycle. Recycle paper and toys as well as clothes. Consider the energy-conscious alternative of bicycling. Not buying more than needed and appropriate is another way of not wasting the earth's resources!
- Take nature walks with the children. Enjoy the beauty of the trees or of whatever form of nature is around you. Think about and share lessons nature offers us.
- Investigate with your children your heritage. Perhaps learn about your ancestors' relationship with nature and crafts. If there are old legends, enjoy some of them.
- Find ways to be simple, natural and economical. Perhaps you would like to investigate nutritional values of products. What happens when something is refined?

Parent Values Activities

- Discuss together the messages of the advertisements you see in your daily life. Ask, *"What do you think the message is?"* Listen to your children's thoughts. Give them time to process the messages. Have fun coming up with what nature's message might be.

# TOLERANCE

## For Parents of Two- Through Seven-Year-Olds

### At Group Meetings

- Review the Tolerance Points in *Living Values Activities for Children Ages 3–7* so parents can hear how different aspects of tolerance can be explained to children that age.
- In the parent group, review the activity, Liking Myself—Even When I Make a Mistake (*Living Values Activities for Children Ages 3–7*).
- Ask the parents to form groups of three. Each caregiver can take a turn correcting another who is playing the role of a child who has made a mistake. Give each other feedback about how it feels to be the child, and share as a group ways you've found to give supportive corrections.
- Sing a song about a rainbow. Ask the parents to list the different races, cultures and groups in your country. Ask, *"Are there prejudices in our country? How can we become more appreciative of the beauty of the rainbow? How can we teach our children to be more appreciative?"*
- Read folk tales and favorite stories about the variety of cultures in your country. Discuss the strengths and beauties of different cultures.

## At Home

- Read folk tales of your own heritage to your children. Read stories from other cultures. Talk positively about the qualities we need for a better world and your desire for a better world. Say that many people share a desire for a better world. Talk to your children about the people in the world as our family.
- Include all people of the world in your prayers with the children at night.
- Make or sample food from different cultures.
- Make positive comments about specific people of different races, religions or cultures as you and the children encounter them during the week.

# For Parents of Children Eight Years and Older

## At Group Meetings

- Discuss the Tolerance Reflection Points from *Living Values Activities for Children Ages 8–14.*
- Have parents review A Lack of Tolerance and the awareness activities (*Living Values Activities for Children Ages 8–14*). They might wish to answer some of the questions listed in the second awareness activity. Ask parents to share their experiences of when they first became aware of discrimination or of what it felt like to be discriminated against. Discuss different forms of discrimination—based on race, religion, gender, wealth, education, beauty, etc. Ask parents to share stories and folk tales which were powerful in creating a difference in their own perceptions.
- Review the Rainbow concept (*Living Values Activities for Children Ages 8–14*) and the activities the students will be doing. Ask parents to generate ideas on how we can help ourselves and others become more appreciative of diversity, more appreciative of the beauty of the rainbow.

- Read folk tales and favorite stories about the variety of cultures in your country. Discuss the strengths and beauties of the different cultures. (Share some of those stories with your children.)

## At Home

- Speak positively to your children about your own heritage and the heritage of others. Become aware of and frown upon racist jokes or of making fun in subtle ways of other cultures or races. Be aware of the tendency to scapegoat during times when there are perceptions of scarcity. Think about how you wish to react. Not participating is one option. Telling the negative joke teller that you find it offensive is another. A third option is saying you like people of that race—and stating a few qualities you have found in people of that race. Your children will learn tolerance most rapidly by your example.

- Talk positively about the qualities, needs and desires for a better world that we all share. Talk to your children about the people in the world as "our family."

- Include all people of the world in your prayers with the children.

- Teach tolerance of life's inconveniences with a light attitude and words of understanding.

# COOPERATION

## For Parents of Two- Through Seven-Year-Olds

### At Group Meetings

- Review Cooperation Points in the *Living Values Activities for Children Ages 3–7* so parents can hear how cooperation is explained to children that age.
- Review the Cooperative Eating exercise in the children's unit. Get parents to play this game, but their activity should be different from the children's. They can only give one bite to one person, and then must feed everyone in the group with their elbows straight before getting back to that person. In the spirit of play, it should be great fun!
- Have parents tell their favorite stories about cooperation.
- Sing "The Star Song."
- Have parents cooperatively build houses out of Lego bricks, blocks or milk containers. Discuss. Ask, *"Which types of behaviors and words help the feeling of cooperation? Which behaviors and words detract from the feeling of cooperation?"*
- Do one of the Together We Can exercises (*Living Values Activities for Children Ages 3–7*).

### At Home

- Read stories about cooperation to the children.
- When you are preparing to go on a picnic, go to the park or do something fun, ask everyone in the family to tell you how they can cooperate.

Parent Values Activities

If the two-year-old cannot think of a way to help, create a task for him or her to do.

- Enjoy doing small, cooperative things to make the world a better place. For instance, place a neighbor's paper on their porch when it is wet outside, take someone a meal that you cooked together or plant a flower in a little pot for someone who has been loving.
- Notice and positively comment on the children's cooperative behavior.
- Remark to your children when you notice how someone is cooperating with your family. Perhaps an uncle noticed the plants were thirsty and watered them, maybe a neighbor helped get the children to school or someone fed the dog while you were away.
- When you are out with your children, point out examples of cooperation. For example, how the farmer, the truck driver and the grocer each does his or her part so there is food; how everyone on the rowing team cooperates to speed the boat in the right direction.

# For Parents of Children Eight Years and Older

## At Group Meetings

- Discuss the Cooperation Reflection Points (*Living Values Activities for Children Ages 8–14*).
- Ask parents to review the children's activities. Play a couple of cooperative games. Have parents try the Cooperative Eating exercise (*Living Values Activities for Children Ages 8–14*). But change the rules so they can only give one bite to one person, and then must feed everyone in the group with their elbows straight before getting back to that person. With the spirit of play, it should be great fun.

- Ask the parents to tell their favorite stories about cooperation.
- Allow parents to build a tower out of newspaper cooperatively. Discuss which types of behaviors and words help the feeling of cooperation and which ones detract from the feeling.
- Discuss *attitude* as the most important ingredient in cooperation. Think about the saying, "Cooperation follows love." The dynamics of anger, guilt, resentment and blaming are easily tied in when there is expectation, disappointment, nagging and demands.

## At Home

- Make sure that play time is still in your schedule with the children.
- When you are preparing to go on a picnic, go to the park, go camping or do something fun, ask everyone in the family to tell you how they can cooperate.
- Ask for cooperation when you need it. Tell them you appreciate their cooperation.
- When the children ask for your cooperation, see if it is possible, and do it affectionately.
- Enjoy doing small cooperative things together to make the world a better place. Compliment the children when they independently do kind things for others.
- Notice and positively comment on the children's cooperative behavior.
- Remark to your children when you notice how someone is cooperating with your family.

# FREEDOM

## For Parents of Infants Through Seven-Year-Olds

Freedom is not included in *Living Values Activities for Children Ages 3–7*, as it is caregivers who give the infants, toddlers, and young children the experience of freedom. Children naturally know how to be free. They simply need an environment which supports and allows freedom and is responsive to the joy of being. Create the physical and emotional space for them to play and be. Enjoy playing and being free with them! Respect their emotions and simple requests. Give them choices as they grow. Be sensible; do not allow too much freedom without discipline. Each age has its own accomplishments and skills to learn.

## For Parents of Children Eight Years and Older

### At Group Meetings

- Present the Freedom Reflection Points (*Living Values Activities for Children Ages 8–14*).
- The parents may wish to discuss these points and add their own.
- Form a circle. Ask each parent/caregiver to finish the sentences, *"I feel lucky I have the freedom to . . . I wish all people had the freedom to . . ."* (as in the Favorite Famous Freedom Lines activity (*Living Values Activities for Children Ages 8–14*).
- Ask members of the group to talk about inner freedom. Discuss the questions in the Values Activities (*Living Values Activities for Children Ages 8–14*).
- Show the parents the activities in the ages eight through fourteen section. Look at the discussion of the Freedom Reflection Points and A Slice of

History. Both sections deal with freedoms and responsibilities. Discuss how that applies at home. The discussion may open concerns parents have with children in this age range, as often children want more freedoms than are appropriate for their age and want to have less than their share of responsibility. If parents are having problems at home, the facilitator may want to address some of those concerns during this section and again during the Responsibility section.

- Have a good time creating a "living sculpture" of inner freedom.

## At Home

- Play and spend time with your children every day. Enjoy them and yourself!
- Think about age-appropriate tasks for your children. Assign a couple, if they do not have any. Positively affirm their efforts and contributions. When they want more rights, assign appropriate responsibility. If they let go of a responsibility to which they had committed, calmly have a chat. Discuss alternatives, listen while they share feelings, share your own feelings. Make a plan together that meets both your needs.
- Enjoy a day with the family.

# UNITY

# For Parents of Two- Through Seven-Year-Olds

## At Group Meetings

- Review the Unity Points in *Living Values Activities for Children Ages 3–7* so parents can hear how unity is explained to children that age.

- Ask parents to find stories about unity in their culture and to share with other parents.
- Review the children's activities. (Don't try the Musical Squat—it's much easier for four-year-olds, as they are much closer to the floor.)

## At Home

- Read stories about unity to your children.
- Observe the geese in the sky or other animals who display unity.
- Positively remark when the family is working on something together. Say, *"It feels good to have unity."*
- When you are out with your children, point out examples of unity. For example, how firefighters work together to put out a fire, how the soccer team works together to get the ball to the goal, etc.
- Arrange a family meeting and determine if there's something you would all like to do differently as a family. Identify that common goal, then accomplish it with a sense of unity and togetherness. For instance, you may all like to eat dinner together several nights a week, play together on Saturday afternoon or be extra loving to Sally because she needs extra support now.

# For Parents of Children Eight Years and Older

## At Group Meetings

- Discuss the Unity Reflection Points from *Living Values Activities for Children Ages 8–14.*
- Ask parents to find stories about unity in their culture and to share with other parents.

- Review the children's activities. Enjoy a circle dance together.
- Discuss a shared goal, hope or vision of your parent group—something members feel would make something closer to the way they want it to be. Think about ideas, and then make a plan to put it into action. It could be a non-physical plan, such as members deciding they will be friendly to every child they see.

## At Home

- Observe the geese in the sky or other animals who display unity. Explore the cultures of unity in animals. Create the opportunity for your children to investigate these, or investigate them together, and then ask them to read the stories to you.
- Notice positive examples of unity in the news, in the neighborhood and in everyday life. Share stories of unity that you know.
- If your child is involved in a project at school, and all of a sudden his or her attitude changes from positive to negative, check on the appreciation level of the group at school. Think together about some of the Reflection Points, such as: Unity continues by accepting and appreciating each person and his or her contribution. One note of disrespect can cause unity to be broken. Talk about what is causing a change, and discuss what is needed to create unity again.
- Arrange a family meeting and determine if there's something you would all like to do differently as a family. Identify that common goal, then accomplish it with a sense of unity and togetherness.

# SECTION THREE

## Parenting Skills

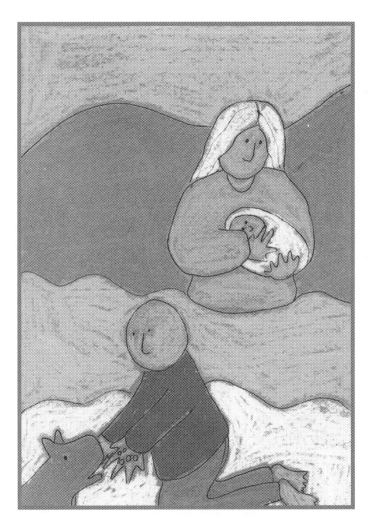

The following parenting skills can be taught in response to situations that may be creating obstacles for the parent in imparting values.

Alternatively, the facilitator may choose to teach one skill or awareness at each of the sessions, depending on the needs of the parents.

PARENT CONCERN:

## *"I don't have enough time."*

PARENTING SKILL 1

# The Importance of Play and "Us Time"

# For Parents of Infants Through Four-Year-Olds

As most parents will agree, children of this age require an inordinate amount of attention. Time to cuddle, hold, play and attend to the child is invaluable. It is said that play is the work of the child. Play is the child's opportunity to experience freedom, joy and self-expression. It is a time when children can feel "full of themselves." Children work out their feelings in play, and if there have been traumatic experiences, play is healing. Play is a time of learning and growing cognitively, emotionally, socially, spiritually and physically. As a parent, playing with your children creates a cooperative, loving, and close bond and adds to the joy within the relationship.

Enter into their world. Play at their level and pace. Join the world of pretend. When they pretend to give you a bite of food, pretend to give them a bite. Play with clay and blocks, with dolls and trucks, play peek-a-boo and roll around on the floor. Play with balls, rolling them initially. When a child structures a game and is enjoying it, do not come along and make it harder so he or she is not successful. Simply be—accepting, reflecting, enjoying.

# For Parents of Five- to Nine-Year-Olds

Yes, it's hard to find time in this busy world for play and values activities. But, ask yourself:

- Why did I have children in the first place?
- Why do I love them?
- What do I wish I had done more of over the past few years?

Finding some time every day to play with your children is so important. That precious time is when relationships are enjoyed and the feelings of love grow. The children who get "Us Time" get that full attention and close eye contact which tells them they are valued and valuable.

Ask yourself:

- What do I enjoy doing myself that I can do with my child?
- What would be fun for both myself and the child?

There's an interesting saying: "Cooperation follows love." By playing every day with your children so they can count on getting your full, undivided attention for even fifteen minutes a day, minor negativities will simply disappear. Play games you enjoyed at that age or would have liked to have played. Play pretend games, play outside, play with balls and dolls, play with the simple enjoyment of enjoying your children. Introduce them to the common games of your culture—perhaps cards and board games, soccer or circle dances. Don't get competitive yourself, but model graceful winning and losing. (Winning a game with a child about one-third of the time is fine.) Teach them things; allow them to experience themselves as successful. Take them places that are free. Go on a walk to a park, a lake or the ocean.

Plan how you can build in fifteen minutes per day with each of your two children. If you have six children, can you devote an hour to play or Us Time? Play cooperative games as a group where everyone wins. Us Time can also be a time of just listening with your full attention. Use daily routine time to interact with your children. For instance, converse in the bus or car or as you walk to the store.

# For Parents of Ten- to Eighteen-Year-Olds

The same applies to older children as it does for younger children, so ask yourself the questions listed above.

Finding quality time every day to be with your children is critical to the success of your relationships with them. Even giving fifteen minutes of your full attention, chatting with them about their day, stopping what you are doing to really be there will make a difference. It is said that a thirteen-year-old needs as much attention as a five-year-old. With peer pressure what it is today, a key safety net is a good relationship between parent and child. If the communication channels are open and the feelings of love and closeness are there, some of the turbulence of teenage years can be avoided. Additionally, when the child is in conflict, he or she is more likely to come to you for advice than to seek out peers. Find something that both you and your child like doing, even if it's a short walk around the block. By

*Parenting Skills*

consistently giving them the regard and love involved in Us Time, they will feel better about themselves, and they (and you) will navigate the teenage years more easily.

PARENT CONCERN:

*"He always seems to do things to
get my negative attention."*

*"She doesn't like praise."*

---

PARENTING SKILL 2

# Encouragement and Positively Building Behaviors

---

# For Parents of All Age Groups

Children love the attention of parents. However, if they can't get your attention by doing something positive, they may seek your negative attention. Negative attention is better than no attention at all. At least with negative attention they know they have made an impact, they have had an effect, they are alive. The problem with giving more than twenty seconds of negative attention—such as screaming or bawling out a child—is after a short period of time, the negative behavior increases. It also serves to build into your relationship more dynamics of blame, guilt, anger and resentment.

It takes less time and less emotional energy to pay positive attention, encourage and positively reinforce behaviors.

- What do your children do well?
- What do they do consistently without being reminded?
- Do these areas receive your praise?

Children usually do well in the areas in which they receive positive affection and praise. People like attention, love and respect. Children tend to do the things that earn those responses—if those positives are available.

Praise is usually a positive reinforcer for most children. When they experience something positive for a particular behavior, that behavior increases. You can tell if your praise or affirmation is a positive experience for your child by watching if the behavior increases. However, there may be other responses to watch for. For example, some children don't seem to like praise and look sour when they get it. They may have found the praise embarrassing. Others don't seem to accept it. They simply do not believe you—perhaps you said it was *"great"* and they do not think so. A few children occasionally get worse immediately after praise, such as a boy who usually hits his sister after being praised for being *"such a terrific young man"* when he stops for a few minutes. So why does he immediately hit her again? It is likely he is accustomed to getting so much negative feedback in that area that the positive feedback is anxiety-provoking. He elected to finish the anxiety as soon as possible.

A few simple rules for giving affirmations, praise and positively building behaviors make the process rewarding for both parent and child.

## 1. Give specific praise and affirmations.

That means use descriptive words. For example, a five-year-old will appreciate and believe your saying, *"You made the back of that 'B' straight and just the right size."* He can observe the "B." However, he may not take as much benefit from your saying, *"You have the best printing in the whole wide world."* A three-year-old girl with a just-done painting is quite happy with a description accompanied with smiles and loving eye contact: *"Wow, look at all the colors you used—red and blue and purple! And there are all sorts of circles and lines!"* It is also reinforcing to children to have their efforts recognized: *"You listened to Guillermo when he really needed you to listen. That was being a friend."*

## 2. Give specific praise, and then add a quality that will build on values.

For example, *"I liked the way you just helped your little sister. You were giving happiness."* Or, *"You didn't hit when he called you a name. You stayed in your self-respect and power. Good for you!"* Or, *"Thank you for putting away your things so quickly. That was great cooperation."* Or, *"I like the way you thought about it and were able to stop and say 'arms are for hugging, not for shoving.' That was choosing peace."*

Children remember when you say they have these qualities. As these qualities become part of their self-perception, their self-esteem grows.

## 3. The praise must be genuine.

The person receiving the praise will know if it is not sincere. Delight in the person, appreciative eye contact and respect are invaluable indicators of sincerity, easily perceived by two-year-olds or eighteen-year-olds. Of course, the manner of delivery needs to be different depending on the age. Cooing is great for babies, gushing for most two- to four-year-old girls. Boys tend to prefer praise delivered in a matter-of-fact way, especially after age eight. Many teenagers are like soft-boiled eggs: hard on the outside, soft on the inside. They may not seem to notice your praise—may shrug it off the hard exterior—but you know it has been effective when that behavior increases, when they start hanging around you more and when the hard facade fades.

## 4. Praise always leaves a positive feeling within the receiving person.

Ensure that your praise, affirmations or encouraging words do just that. That is, do not end praise with a "spoiler." For example, how does the husband feel when the wife says, *"Honey, you did a great job cleaning the garage. It looks so organized. I don't know why you don't keep it like that all the time. It's always such a mess!"* That was a spoiler! Or when the husband says to the wife, *"What a delicious dessert that was! Why can't you make something like that more often?"* Or when the parent says to the child, *"It was fun working with you today. You concentrated and finished your homework quickly. If you'd only do that all the time, it wouldn't be such a hassle every day. You are usually so irresponsible."* The praise started out great, but the comments turned negative and the positive feelings were ruined. People do not need praise or affirmations all the time. But, when you do speak, what is the effect of your words?

## 5. *When a new behavior is first beginning, praise it immediately.*

It is appropriate to provide immediate feedback for a new positive behavior. Then, as the behavior becomes a habit, gradually reduce encouragement or the praise. Occasionally you might note the continuing effort. *"I appreciate that you've been remembering to tell me where you are going every day."*

PARENT CONCERN:
## *"All they want to do is watch TV."*
## *"They love these violent videos."*

---

PARENTING SKILL 3
# The Balance of Discipline and Love

---

Almost all parents recognize the importance of a healthy diet. They want their children to have nourishing meals and develop good eating habits. They carefully choose the food the family eats. Food for the mind is important as well. The diet of what children watch on television affects their minds and attitudes. Research has shown that more than four hours of television per day is actually harmful to children. They do not develop as well physically or in expressive language, creativity or social skills. Television can be addictive; it can be a "mind robber." One can sit in front of the television and simply have the mind filled. Emotions we choose to ignore can be dismissed, and we do not have to interact with others or use our mind to find something to do. Many children, consequently, have limited time for the essential tasks of childhood which are critical for physical, cognitive, emotional, spiritual and social growth. It is important for children to play and exercise, to create and invent, to relate and express.

In the same way that some sweets are okay in a diet, a bit of television is okay, depending on the content. Violence teaches violence. Part of becoming a parent with the balance of discipline and love is learning that it is appropriate to have sensible rules and to tell the children what is right and wrong.

Talking about right and wrong actions is most often accepted when the parent is able to share that information calmly and with love. It is amazing how children accept sensible rules. They may fuss for a few days, but you will see positive changes. It is wise to monitor the television and videos to which children are exposed, just as it is wise to monitor the environments in which they are placed. Give small doses of the best of television. There are a few beautiful programs that are inspiring, funny, creative and humanizing. There are informational ones that are interesting and educational.

Allow your children the opportunities to build forts, climb trees, play sports, dance, do puzzles and read. Read with your children story books and wonderful tales before bedtime. Talk with them and enjoy your children. This does require more time on the part of the parent, but because of your encouragement and extra effort, your children will learn to entertain themselves, be more creative and positive and play more successfully with others.

PARENT CONCERN:

## *"He gets so angry with his teachers."*
## *"She feels so sad when she gets rejected."*

---

PARENTING SKILL 4

# Active Listening

---

Sometimes parents feel helpless when their children feel badly about peer problems at school, or when they are upset with friends, coaches or teachers. Caregivers often jump to sympathize, admonish or give advice. Or, they get angry with the child for being angry with an authority figure.

Think about when you are really upset with someone, and another person jumps in, immediately telling you what to do or how silly you are being. Chances are you don't feel better. But a quiet chat with an understanding friend allows us to process what happened. Listening on the part of a patient, loving person is an invaluable gift. Reflecting the feelings of children allows them to accept and "own" their emotions. As emotions are accepted, they gradually reduce in intensity. For example, when someone really listens, a child will frequently move from anger at an authority figure to talking about how his or her feelings have been hurt.

The process of being listened to allows children to feel valued, which allows them to accept their own hurt and to look at the overall situation with more understanding. And, after having been listened to, occasionally one small sentence of advice is accepted. Or, this is also an opportunity to say, *"What other way could you have handled it?"* As children are encouraged to think and generate alternatives, the likelihood increases of their being able to act in a fashion that does not cause sorrow to themselves or others next time.

One of the most effective tools of listening is called active listening. Active listening is reflecting back the content and emotions that the other person is communicating—without sounding like a parrot. It requires taking the time to really listen and having an accepting, loving attitude. The listener's reactions are not interjected, nor are questions asked. It does require practice. Example: A child crying over being called a name: *"She called me ugly."* Parent: *"It really hurt your feelings to have her call you a name."*

PARENT CONCERN:

## *"There's been so much change and the kids feel so insecure."*

---

PARENTING SKILL 5

# Establishing a Ritual

---

Children, especially little ones, often feel insecure when there is change. Divorces are very difficult for all. Moving, the parent switching to different work hours, the death of a relative, etc., can make very real differences in the life of a child and in a family. Explain to the child what is happening. For small children, keep it simple. It is important to explain to children as young as eighteen months why one parent or grandparent is not there. For all children, keep it healthy, i.e., do not label your now-separating spouse as a liar or cheat.

With a change, some children become withdrawn and depressed, others whine or become aggressive. When there is turmoil, the usual routines can stop. Re-establish routines and develop rituals. A routine may be making the beds in the morning, having a certain drink, saying a blessing before breakfast. Or perhaps a snack after school, or a chance to play with dad before or after dinner. A ritual may be a set bedtime, a bedtime story told on the bed with the children cuddled around and maybe a goodnight prayer. These can help immensely. Keep the rules consistent. Children feel reassured and secure with routine.

PARENT CONCERN:

## *"I say 'no,' and he keeps at me until I give in."*

---

PARENTING SKILL 6

# Think Before Saying No

---

Sometimes we say "no" quickly. We are busy and don't want to be bothered. But frequently the parent feels guilty later on when the child continues to want to do it, and it seems like it would be fine at that later time. When the child asks to do it again and the parent gives in, the child has learned that asking repetitively works. Some ask forty times before the exasperated parent gives in! Think before you say no. Would it be good for the child? Can you take a few minutes now? It may take two minutes longer to let the child stir the cookie batter if he or she wants to do that, but it helps the child develop age-appropriate skills, he or she feels proud of the accomplishment and a feeling of cooperative helping grows. If you do not have the time now, and you would like to say "yes" to the child's request, think about when you would have time. Can you do it in thirty minutes? If your answer is "no," stick to it. Children listen well to parents who say what they mean, stick to what they say and do what they say. Keep your promises.

PARENT CONCERN:

## *"I want my child to be peaceful, but I'm not so peaceful myself."*
## *"I'm just out of energy."*

---

PARENTING SKILL 7

# Time to Be

---

To teach values effectively means we have to have and apply them. To be perfectly honest, this is difficult at times. Most of us want to be peaceful and loving and happy. However, most of us have an off mood or an off day when we feel turmoil, depressed or angry—time when we don't feel good within.

Take some time to be. Be gentle to the self. Spend time with your spouse to keep your marital relationship healthy. Create time to do something that is nourishing for you. Spend a few silent moments in the morning and evening thinking about the day and recharging the self. Parenting is imparting to your children a way of "being." You may not realize how they are adopting your way of communicating and being until they are much older. Parenting is one of the most demanding tasks in the world—and one of the most valuable.

PARENT CONCERN:

*"They don't do anything I ask them to do."*
*"Sometimes they all drive me nuts."*
*"I worry about her constantly."*

---

PARENTING SKILL 8

# Staying Stable and Loving, and Communicating

---

# For Parents of Infants to Seven-Year-Olds

Sometimes it is hard to be patient. Life in this world today places demands on all parents. Being a single parent compounds the demands and the responsibilities. The children constantly want attention, and some do not seem to want to do anything alone. Children will seemingly find a way to fuss, manipulate, or pretend they cannot do something to get the attention—all when you don't feel there is any more to give. Parents often rush, tell children what to do as they quickly pass through a room, and go on. After fifteen requests to do something, most parents become frustrated. Often parents find themselves speaking a lot louder than they wish. Many complain, *"Why do my children only listen when I scream at them?"* Perhaps it's time to get some extra rest, but it may also be time to look at what is happening.

Many children have learned they can ignore parents who are speaking in a normal tone of voice, as the parent soon goes off on his or her own way. The children can simply continue to do what they are enjoying without interrupting the activity. However, they remain alert to the parent's voice tone and know when they had better start complying with that request. They know at which tone a threat will become a reality.

Sometimes the more we rush, the worse things get. The next time you want your child to do something, pause, get within a couple of feet of your child, look at him or her with friendly eye contact and say what you want done. You might gently touch his or her shoulder as you ask. When the task is done, make a positive remark or thank the child for doing it so quickly. Children will figure out that you are paying attention to what you say to them. If the task is not done, return to the child, get close physically and chat about what you wish them to do. Follow through.

As a rule of thumb, think about what you realistically want them to do at that time, communicate that clearly and positively and follow up. Refrain from nagging. Be selective about giving directions; it is irritating to receive constant instructions about things they already do. As they improve in follow-through, you can gradually stop positively affirming every time, but occasionally remark how responsible they are being and positively recognize their contribution.

Sometimes children may not want to study, eat meals or do their chores. They may not want to go to bed on time, or they may wish to watch six hours of television a day. They may be upset over the death of a relative, a change in schools or an upcoming move. Sit down and calmly explain, in simple terms, what is happening or why something is important. Children can understand things when they are very young. Listen to their concerns.

When you are teaching them to do something, do it patiently, pay attention to the interaction and ensure they feel successful when it is done satisfactorily. Plan a few extra minutes so that if something is spilled or something needs to be redone, you can be patient. Notice their skill level so you do not make the task too difficult. Their feeling of success is extremely important in their own perception of their capability. When you do new tasks together, such as learning letters and numbers, make it fun. Use different methods, ask them to draw it, trace it, draw it in the air, sing it. When they ask to play school with you, you have created a great attitude for learning.

Slowing down in between the moments . . . being stable and loving . . . gets more done . . . and it's a lot more fun.

# For Parents of Eight-Year-Olds to Young Adults

At times, it's very difficult to traverse the stages of growing up with each of your children. We hear about the terrible two's and the teenage years, but it seems we are unprepared for the worry we experience over their feelings of rejection, difficulty with peers, poor reading skills, poor choices of friends, illnesses, etc. We are not prepared for the irritation and despair we feel over their sloppy rooms, strange manner of dressing, and lack of interest in the "right things."

Worry and irritation only make the situation worse. With worry comes heaviness. Irritation infuses an angry, demanding tone into the relationship. It is easier to stay stable and loving when we recognize it is just a phase the child is going through, it can be successfully dealt with and we can do that by staying content within the self and giving regard to the child when possible. It seems that each child has a lesson to teach us. Think about your own childhood. How would you have liked your parents to act in any given situation? Ask yourself, what is the lesson to be learned from this child? The difficult or rebellious stage will only be prolonged by our anger and despair. Detach. Try to see the child as who he or she is within and ignore the outside.

It is possible to get beyond your reaction to your son or daughter dressing as a punk rocker. You can continue to treat him or her like a respected human being by seeing the positive qualities inside. With detachment from the situation and a focus on love, it is easier to send good wishes and to maintain a healthy relationship. In the atmosphere of love, a person can more easily do what is good.

Watch the amount of corrections and negative comments on your part. They can destroy the relationship and increase the unhappiness of both you and the child and his or her feelings of unworthiness. Do not nag. Instead, discuss it, and find a solution together. Provide small, logical consequences, when necessary. Often, you can ask the child what a small consequence should be. For example, if young teenagers are piling their clothes on the floor, you might want to discuss with them your feelings, and generate possible solutions together. One solution might be that it is time for them to do their own washing and ironing for a week. Together, decide on a plan that is acceptable to both of you. Try it for a week. Talk again, and see if you are both happy with the results. If not, problem solve again.

Sometimes teenagers make mistakes. (Adults do as well!) When there is a behavior you are really concerned about, such as stealing, it is time to really think, and talk. Think about your values and what you want for your son or daughter. When you are calm, and can be serious but loving, sit down with him or her. Tell him that you love him very much and you are very concerned about the behavior. Then tell him why. For example, from a father to his son, *"To me, integrity is the mark of a man. You are getting older now, and I want to talk with you about why I think honesty is so important. When you are honest, you are. . . ."* Punishment sometimes appears effective for a few days, but the long-term result is more resentment, anger and retaliation. If you communicate lovingly when your pre-teen is having a problem, if he has a problem as a teenager, he is much more likely to come to you for advice.

Spend time, play, talk and choose well your rare words of advice—when the ears are most receptive. Good luck!

*Parenting Skills*

PARENT CONCERN:

## *"They're always fighting. It disrupts even the fun activities."*

PARENTING SKILL 9

# "Time-Out" to Think and Communicate

# Time-Out

Time-Out is a method used when children behave inappropriately. They are asked to go to another room or sit alone for a short time. It is not considered punishment; it is simply considered the withdrawal of positive reinforcement. The positive reinforcement is the parent's love and/or attention.

The principal reason for implementing Time-Out is that when it is done properly, there is no need for punitive measures. This fits in well with a values-based approach as the goal is to get out of the cycle of feelings of inadequacy, blame, shame, fear, hurt, resentment and retaliation. In fact, when Time-Out is done with a values-based approach, soon there is no need to use this method as the child has begun to think about his or her own behavior, developed more social awareness and is making better choices. This values-based Time-Out is being called "Thinking Time."

Thinking Time is effective with children as young as eighteen months. The time out period can range from part of a minute up to fifteen minutes. Longer than fifteen minutes has been found to be ineffective, as a cycle of resentment is activated.

A way to introduce Thinking Time as part of a values-based approach is for caregivers to meet with the children and say: *"Families are for giving happiness and love to each other. Sometimes we give happiness to each other and are responsible, and sometimes we give sorrow. When we do that, we need to think about what we can do instead. So, from now on, when someone is giving sorrow, your dad and I (or whoever are the caregivers) will give you this signal (or say _____). That means that you are to take some Thinking Time and sit over there for _____ minutes to think about what you could do or say that would give happiness instead of sorrow."*

For young children, you may want to have a Peace Bear in the corner that will "help" the child think. For little children, start with one minute and gradually increase the time until the child sits for three to five minutes. Sometimes little children do not Time-Out easily. Make Time-Out less "scary" in their eyes. Practice doing a Time-Out when they are feeling good. Lead them gently by the hand. Practice filling the self with peace or a pink bubble of love. When you do ask them to think for a moment, be calm rather than angry, make the Thinking Time place very close to where they are, make sure it is well-lit, decrease the time to a few seconds of his or her being quiet and then gradually increase the time.

For a teenager, the bedroom is often the best place for Thinking Time. For an older child, start with three to five minutes. If a teenager is starting to be rude, you may want to say: *"You seem upset, would you like to take a few minutes to cool down?"* Or perhaps, *"How about a few minutes in your Peace place."*

It is important to Time-Out the child before you are annoyed—that is, when you first notice inappropriate behavior. Time-Out should depend on their behavior, not on your mood. If you do it calmly, they will Time-Out much more easily.

Parenting Skills

After the Thinking Time, help the child create an alternative behavior. Then, you can peacefully ask, *"Were you able to think of a way to give happiness? What could you have done instead of hitting your brother?"* Or, *"Were you able to think of a way to do that differently?"* Positively remark on the child's alternative. The insight and wonderful alternatives that a two-year-old can produce are remarkable! Give the child a hug or a special smile when you see that new behavior.

# Communicate (Steps for Conflict Resolution)

When the parent has time, it is good to have children communicate when they are in conflict. It teaches them to express their feelings and generate win-win solutions. When children are in conflict, sit down with them. The parent could start by saying (pause at ellipse points), *"I don't like hitting or name calling. You can use words to say how you feel and what you like and want. Mark, I want you to start by telling your sister how you feel. . . . Okay, Anne, what did he say? . . . Good sharing how you feel. Anne, how did you feel? . . . Mark, what did she say? . . . You both listened well. Now, Mark, tell Anne what you don't like. . . . Anne, your turn. . . . Mark, what would you like Anne to do instead? . . . What did he say, Anne? . . . Good. Now Anne, what would you like Mark to do instead? . . . What did she say, Mark? . . . Good. Now, can you both do that?"*

If it is a fair suggestion, stop there. If not, ask them to generate another solution. Then, ask them if they can do that for a certain amount of time. Set a short enough time so that they will be successful. Pay some positive attention to each during the practice time. At the end of the time, tell them both what specifically you are pleased about.

To summarize:

Ask each child, *"How do you feel?"*

Each child listens and repeats it back.

State, *"What would you like* _____ *not to do?"*

State, *"What would you like* _____ *to do?"*

Each child listens and repeats it back.

Ask, *"Can you both do that?"*

(Set a short amount of time for them to do that, and praise their success at the end of the time period.)

Both of the above methods focus on developing communication and thinking skills that move children from conflict to peace. The methods also take the parent out of the unenviable position of playing judge and place the parent in the position of a loving, peaceful parent.

# ABOUT THE AUTHOR

**Diane G. Tillman** is a licensed educational psychologist and marriage and family therapist who worked in the California public school system, for twenty-three years. Diane travels widely internationally, lecturing on personal development and training educators. She has worked with LVEP since its inception, and continues to develop content and training materials. She has served with the United Nations Association-USA at the local, regional and national levels.

# ABOUT THE
# LIVING VALUES PROGRAM

**Living Values: An Educational Program** is a partnership among educators around the world. This program is supported by UNESCO, sponsored by the Spanish Committee of UNICEF, the Planet Society, and the Brahma Kumaris, in consultation with the Education Cluster of UNICEF (New York).

Visit the Living Values Web site at: *http://www.livingvalues.net*

# The Living Values Series

The purpose of the *Living Values* series is to provide guiding principles and tools for the development of the whole person, recognizing that the individual is comprised of physical, intellectual, emotional, and spiritual dimensions.

The *Living Values* series offers a variety of experiential activities for teachers and parents to help teach children and young adults to develop twelve critical social values: cooperation, freedom, happiness, honesty, humility, love, peace, respect, responsibility, simplicity, tolerance and unity. In each book, these twelve values are explored using age-appropriate lessons that incorporate group discussions, reading, quiet reflection time, songs, artwork and action-oriented activities.

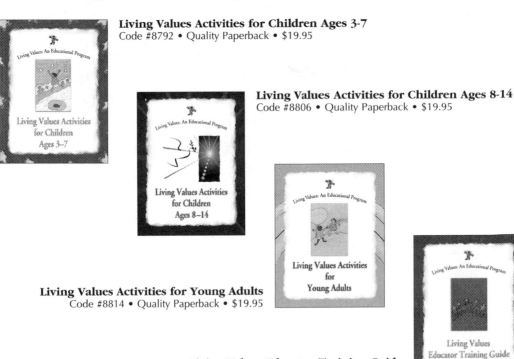

**Living Values Activities for Children Ages 3-7**
Code #8792 • Quality Paperback • $19.95

**Living Values Activities for Children Ages 8-14**
Code #8806 • Quality Paperback • $19.95

**Living Values Activities for Young Adults**
Code #8814 • Quality Paperback • $19.95

**Living Values Educator Training Guide**
Code #8830 • Quality Paperback • $12.95